Introduction _____ 2
Terrarium: A Complete Guide on Terrarium Plants, Ideas & Building Kits 3
    Terrarium Meaning & Definition _____ 4
    Types of Plants for a Terrarium _____ 7
    Terrarium Air Plants _____ 20
    Terrarium Ideas for Inspiration _____ 33
    How to make a Terrarium DIY _____ 41
    The Best Terrarium Kits for Kids and Adults _____ 45
Asked Questions on Terrariums _____ 59
    Happiness in a Terrarium _____ 61
And bonus for you _____ 62
20 Best Terrarium Plants for a Beautiful DIY Terrarium __ 63
    What Are Terrarium Plants? _____ 65
    The Best Terrarium Plants _____ 67
    Open Terrarium Plants _____ 70
    Closed Terrarium Plants _____ 79
    Small Terrarium Plants _____ 88
    Large Terrarium Plants _____ 95
    Caring for Terrarium Plants _____ 103
Where to Buy Terrarium Plants _____ 108
    Terrarium Plants FAQs _____ 113
    Gardening Under a Glass _____ 115

Introduction

A lot of time and work has been invested in this book.
Everything was written with love to bring you knowledge and joy.
I will greatly appreciate your feedback.
Do not pass by, write a review (what do you think) I want to make this book perfect for you!

Terrarium: A Complete Guide on Terrarium Plants, Ideas & Building Kits

A terrarium is a **work of art** and a **thriving environment for plants** two in one. It's easier to maintain than an [aquarium full of fishes](#) and [aquarium greenery](#) and can make any room so much more interesting.

But what exactly is a terrarium and how can you make one?

Read on to find out more about terrariums and all the things that go into them.

Terrarium Meaning & Definition

A terrarium is a **miniature garden growing inside a transparent glass container**. It consists of soil, plants, pebbles, and often, a charcoal layer that keeps the water and the air clean.

The container can be a simple glass jar, a fish tank, or a handcrafted piece of glass. It can also be a transparent non-plastic container, though glass is usually the best choice.

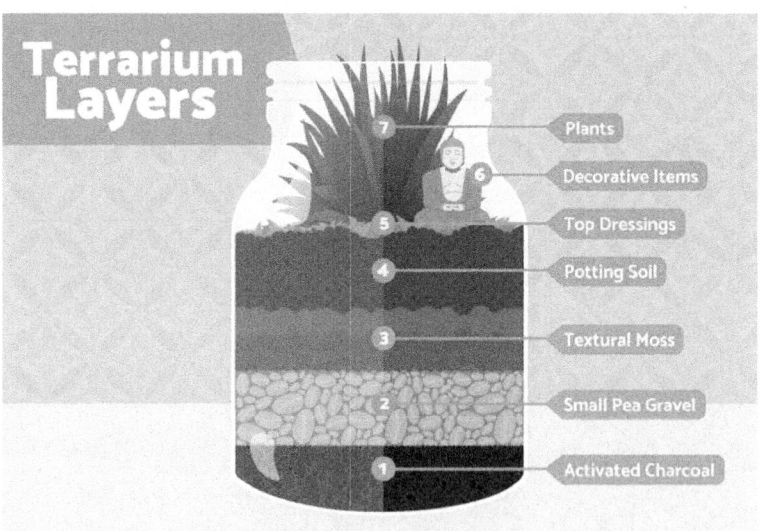

So far so good, but how does it work? It's simple. The plants and the soil in a terrarium **release moisture which condenses on the glass walls** and then returns to the plants.

A terrarium can look very similar to a vivarium. But while the latter serves as a habitat for an animal, **terrariums sustain only plants** and not animals. Terrariums can be open or sealed.

Open Terrarium

Open terrariums offer a **less humid environment with more air circulation**. They facilitate the growth of plants that like drier conditions and are often decorative.

Open terrariums **require careful watering** and a bit more maintenance than sealed ones.

Sealed Terrarium

*Sealed terrariums or closed terrariums are fitted with a lid to create a **self-sufficient ecosystem** with its own water cycle.*

*Plants **recycle the nutrients they take from soil** and release moisture which returns to the soil. Sealed terrariums **don't usually require watering**.*

Types of Plants for a Terrarium

Plants are the key constituents of a terrarium. The thing to remember is that some types of plants do better in an enclosed glass jar than others. Here are a couple of other things to consider.

- Size – The best plants for your terrarium are small enough to fit into it without touching the walls of the container.
- Moisture – Plants that like moist soil tend to do well in a terrarium, especially in a sealed one.
- Foliage – Leafy plants add color and vibrancy to your glass container all-year-long.
- Light – It's prudent to avoid plants with different light requirements. If some plants prefer shade while others need bright sunlight every day, it can be hard to maintain healthy growing conditions for both.
- Care – Undemanding plants are best for a terrarium since you don't want to fuss over them all the time and disturb their arrangement.

Considering these factors, succulents and air plants tend to be the best plants for a terrarium.

Succulents for a Terrarium

Succulents store water in their leaves and stem, hence their name. They are adapted to growing in dry soil that doesn't get much rain. They can **thrive in low-moisture environments**.

That said, <u>succulents</u> still need a bit of water to keep on growing. They also like warm temperatures—the cold easily damages them.

Important: Succulents grow best in **open terrariums with good air circulation**. Closed terrariums tend to be too humid for these plants.

Succulents is a broad term that contains many families of plants, including <u>Asphodelaceae</u>, <u>Crassulaceae</u>, or <u>Echeveria</u> plants. Cacti are succulents too, though often they are mentioned separately.

Take a look at it now to see some of the most beautiful and interesting succulents you can add to your terrarium.

Aloe Vera (*<u>Asphodelaceae</u>*)

Famed for its healing and soothing sap, the Aloe Vera plant can add a sharp texture to your terrarium. But more than growing it for its looks, you can use its sap to <u>treat small wounds</u>.

Tip: <u>Aloe Vera</u> thrives in the sun, so make sure your terrarium gets plenty of light. Also, be careful not to overwater it—let the soil dry out between waterings.

Sweetheart Hoya (*<u>Hoya kerrii</u>*)

Sweetheart Hoya grows heart-shaped leaves, hence its name. It has the characteristically green vibe of succulents and their low maintenance requirements.

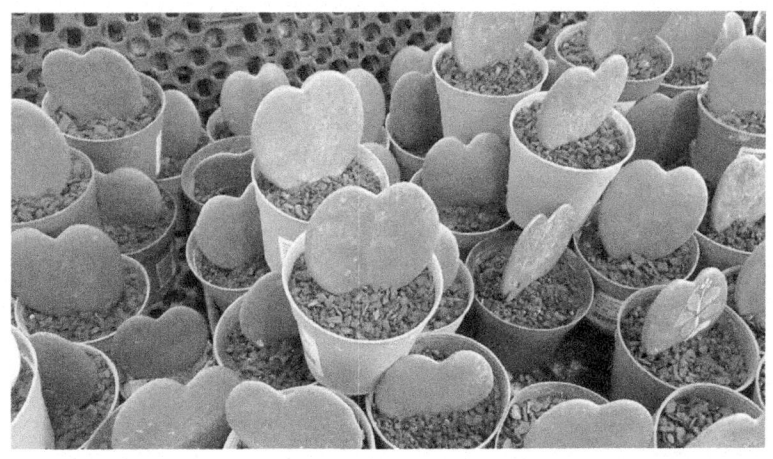

Pincushion Cactus (*Mammillaria* crinita)

The Pincushion Cactus is prickly in a beautiful way, especially when it's adorned with colorful flowers. You have lots of varieties to choose from depending on the size of your glass container.

Tip: *Choose a simple variety for a more rugged look or opt for a flowering hybrid to add color to your terrarium.*

Hens and Chicks (*Sempervivum tectorum*)

This stonecrop plant consists of a main plant and small offspring buds around it which give it its name. It's an all-time favorite for terrariums. No surprise there since it's undemanding, richly textured, and easy to plant and grow.

Paddle Plant (*Kalanchoe thyrsiflora*)

The flat petals of the Paddle Plant grow in a beautiful rosette that makes it a pretty sight in any terrarium. The petals wear different shades of green and can be tinged with red or pink. The Paddle Plant comes in many varieties, giving you lots of options to choose from.

Tip: *Don't let the soil get soggy—the Paddle Plant is susceptible to rot! Also, it needs plenty of light to thrive but best avoid direct exposure to the sun.*

Zebra Haworthia (*Haworthiopsis attenuata*)

This cute succulent plant has horizontal zebra-looking stripes which give it a distinctive look. Zebra Haworthia can reach up to 20" but you can find small varieties no bigger than 3".

This is a resilient plant that can add a rich texture to your arrangement. Zebra Haworthia is by no means boring!

Tip: *In an open terrarium, use the soak and dry watering method to ensure this plant thrives.*

String of Pearls (*Senecio rowleyanus*)

Green beads hang from the long, trailing stems of this delicate and unusual plant. This succulent can produce small, fragrant white flowers, hence another reason to add it to your terrarium.

String of Pearls looks great in a hanging or cascading arrangement. You can also drape it around other decorative elements in your terrarium for special effect.

Agave (*Victoriae reginae*)

Agave comes in so many varieties that you're bound to find one that can fit even an odd spot. Most of the time, though, you'll want to place this plant in the middle of the arrangement where it gets the attention it deserves.

Tip: *Give it as much light as possible. It's the best way to ensure it thrives.*

Tiger Jaws (*Faucaria tigrina*)

The unique, jaw-like toothed leaves of this plant give it a carnivorous look. But the spines are harmless. And that's not all—Tiger Jaws blooms into a delicate yellow flower.

If you're looking for a succulent that can add a dramatic effect to your terrarium, Tiger Jaws could be just perfect for you.

Tip: Don't keep this one in the shade! It needs bright light to thrive.

Burro's Tail (*Sedum morganianum*)

With its beadlike branches and whimsy, trailing stems, Burro's Tail can add a small green cascade to your terrarium. It looks striking in vertical arrangements.

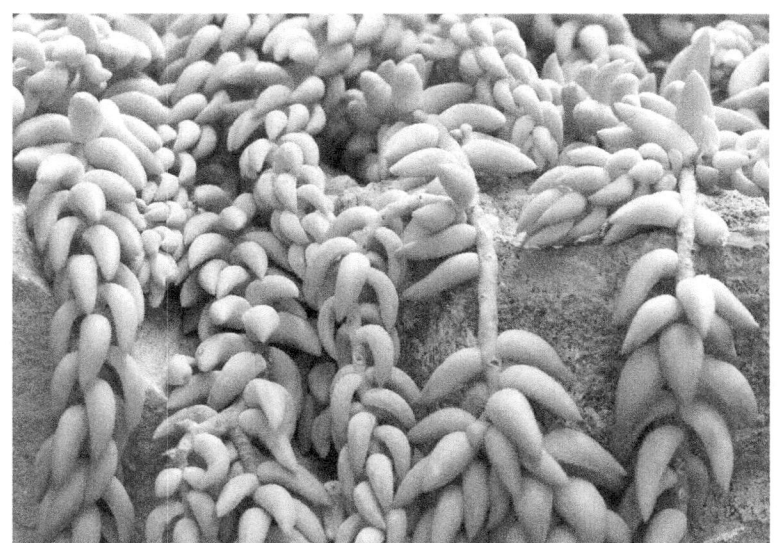

Tip: *Avoid keeping this plant directly in the sun. It grows best in partial sun or bright shade.*

Terrarium Air Plants

Air plants **soak up water and nutrients from the air** through their leaves. Most don't have roots, and those that do use them only to fix themselves to other surfaces. Air plants belong to the Tillandsia genus.

Often striking in appearance, air plants can add a special touch to your terrarium. They are **undemanding** and **can live for years**.

Important: Make sure the base on which you place your air plants is **completely dry**. Most air plants **shouldn't be planted in soil** or sit over a moist surface.

Much like succulents, air plants grow best in an open terrarium. In a closed one, the **high humidity may affect them**.

Explore now some of the most beautiful air plants for your terrarium. You can't go wrong with any of these!

Pink Quill Plant (*Tillandsia cyanea*)

Tillandsia cyanea puts forth interesting purple flowers amid lightweight leaves. When in flower, it's one of the showiest terrarium air plants around.

Tip: *This air plant needs plenty of water to thrive, so make sure to mist it regularly.*

Sky Plant (*Tillandsia ionantha*)

The hardy Tillandsia ionantha is one of the most popular terrarium plants around. It comes in many varieties and impresses with its green explosion of layered leaves. The upper leaves change color from green to red as the plant blooms—it's quite a spectacle!

Tillandsia brachycaulos

Watching Tillandsia brachycaulos grow and bloom is wonderful. That's because the plant turns shades of orange and then red as it blooms.

The leaves of this air plant are not as densely packed as those of other air plants, giving it a light and airy feel. If you want to add grace to your terrarium, it can be an apt choice.

Tillandsia maxima

A stunning choice for larger terrariums, Tillandsia maxima has beautiful coral red leaves and showy purple flowers. It can reach 6" in height and up to 4" in width, making it a striking centerpiece in a spacious terrarium.

Tillandsia capitate

At first glance, this delicate plant looks as if it has been scooped from the bottom of the ocean. But rest assured, it's an air plant.

Its airy, rosette leaves are slender and graceful and turn pink as the flower blooms. <u>Tillandsia capitate</u> has the characteristic purple blooms of other <u>Tillandsia</u> air plants.

Tip: *If you have a small terrarium, look for miniature 3" specimens.*

Tillandsia loliacea

The slender and graceful <u>Tillandsia loliacea</u> is a tiny but charming little plant. Its vivid green leaves and compact, upright growth makes it effortlessly beautiful.

Tillandsia xerographica

This air plant has flat, ribbon-like leaves that curl around each other. Unlike other air plants, it has gray-green leaves that make it a good choice for arrangements with other terrarium air plants.

Tillandsia fuchsii var. garcilis

This delicate, breezy plant may have a bit of a complicated name. But it makes up for it with its thin and lithesome leaves which can spread more widely than other air plants.

Tillandsia kolbii

This air plant grows upright up to 3" tall. Its fuzzy leaves and bluish-purple blooms give it an exotic feel without the fussiness of exotic plants.

Tip: *You don't have to get out of the way to grow this one, just make sure it gets enough sun—bright, indirect light is best.*

Tillandsia stricta

<u>Tillandsia stricta</u> *has huge pink and purple blooms. It's ideal for single specimen terrariums. Its pineapple look gives it a rich texture and creates a beautiful green base for its flowers.*

Terrarium Ideas for Inspiration

Excited already about the idea of having a terrarium? Things get even more exciting when you consider the many different types of terrariums out there. Here are some ideas to inspire you.

Glass Bubble Terrarium

This **classic terrarium shape** will probably never go out of style. Besides, the hole in the side of the container makes it easy to water and rearrange the elements inside if needed. It also provides good ventilation.

Lightbulb Terrarium

The lightbulb terrarium is about as small as terrariums get. You **don't need many materials for this one**, just some tiny plants. And, of course, steady hands. If you like ships-in-a-bottle, you'll love this one.

Coffee Pot Terrarium

*Got an old coffee pot that's gathering dust? Clean it up well and use it as a glass container for plants. This is a great example of how you can **repurpose everyday objects into terrariums**.*

Shot Glass Terrarium

Never had a terrarium before? You can create one in no time with a simple shot glass. You don't have much room in there for plants, so you have to get creative.

Demijohn Terrarium

Got a spare demijohn about the house? You can repurpose it into a large terrarium for succulents. It's not as hard as it may seem.

You just need to use a stick with a blunt end, a thin backscratcher or a similar implement to tamp down the layers inside.

Plants In Egg Shell

Next time you make an omelet, you may want to save the eggshells. Use them as the base for a simple and fun miniature open terrarium.

You can make half a dozen at a time and store them in an egg carton.

Big Jar Terrarium

Keeping things simple is sometimes the best. And the big jar terrarium idea illustrates the point quite well. Pick one with a large neck for excellent ventilation.

Plastic Bottle Terrarium

Glass is usually the material of choice for terrarium containers. But you can also **make a terrarium from a plastic bottle**. Cut the bottle in half to make arranging the plants easier.

Vintage Terrarium

But if you want to give your terrarium a more vintage look, add in some wood. This terrarium idea takes a bit of extra work. But it's well worth the effort, don't you think?

Hanging Jar Lamp Plant Holder

Turning old jars into lamps is cool enough, but why stop there? Add some pebbles and soil and some plants and you can invent a cool terrarium. You won't even have to sun it since the lightbulbs will provide the plants with light.

How to make a Terrarium DIY

Part of the pleasure of owning a terrarium can be making it yourself, with your own hands. Creating a DIY terrarium is a **simple and enjoyable** process.

In fact, it's easier than most people would think. You don't need any previous experience with terrariums, plants, gardening, or landscaping to get started.

Things You'll Need

- A jar or another transparent glass container that lets in light
- Small pebbles for drainage
- Activated charcoal for keeping the water clean and preventing harmful bacteria
- Decorative stones or rocks
- Potting soil, either basic or a special mix for your chosen plants
- Small plants like succulents or air plants
- Basic gardening tools (optional)

Make a Terrarium Step by Step

- Clean the glass container you've chosen if it has seen other uses before.
- Cover the bottom of the container with a 1-2" layer of pebbles to ensure good drainage.
- Add a thin layer of activated charcoal to ward of detrimental bacterial and keep the water within the terrarium fresh.
- Put in the potting soil in a layer at least 2" deep to give the roots plenty of space for support.
- Add the plants, beginning with the largest one. Make a hole in the soil that encloses the roots of the plant and push the plant gently into the soil. If you use air plants, you can skip this step.

- *Arrange the plants creatively. For small terrariums, plant from the back of the container to the front. That way you'll have enough room without hurting the plants.*

- *Decorate the topsoil with pebbles or tiny rocks. You can get creative with this part and add tiny branches and any other decorative features you like.*

- *Lightly water the terrarium.*

- *Place the terrarium where it receives indirect sunlight most of the day. But if your plants have different light requirements, follow those!*

- *For open containers, water regularly before the soil becomes completely dry, usually once every two weeks. For this, you can use a laundry sprinkler or straw.*

- *Sealed containers do not usually require watering. However, you may have to remove the seal to release excess moisture.*

The Best Terrarium Kits for Kids and Adults

If you don't have the materials to build your own terrarium, you can always buy a terrarium kit. Check out the top-rated products below.

Large Glass Succulents Terrarium

This handcrafted large grass terrarium was inspired by the classic look of a Wardian Case. It has a Victorian feel to it that makes it a gorgeous piece of home décor.

You'll like the exquisite detailing and premium quality build. Note that you'll have to buy the plants and soil separately.

Key features:

- Elegant design
- Lead-free solder
- Rust-resistant resin base
- Ideal for succulents

CHECK PRICE

Fairy Garden Terrarium Display Case

Looking for a terrarium with a vintage feel to it? This fairy garden terrarium has a beautiful design and exquisite detailing.

Tip: *While you're at it, you may want to check out some fairy garden ideas.*

The hinged roof allows for easy watering. To use it as an open terrarium, just leave the roof open.

Key features:

- *Prop rod for opening the roof*
- *2" deep tray*
- *Glass accents*
- *Durable build*

CHECK PRICE

Urban Born Glass Terrarium

This eye-catching terrarium brings to mind the greenhouses of centuries past. Stylish yet easy to use, it's an inspired choice for both succulents and air plants.

Key features:

- *Aesthetic design*
- *Handmade glass*
- *Hinged door for easy spraying*
- *Weighs less than 4 pounds*

CHECK PRICE

Bliss Gardens Air Plant Terrarium Kit with Stand

Hanging terrariums add grace to any room, and this air plant terrarium kit proves the point. It comes with an oval glass globe, two air plants, mini rocks, geode crystal, and moss. In short, everything you need to set up a beautiful terrarium in less than an hour.

Key features:

- *Fun hanging design*
- *Ionantha and Caput medusae air plants included*
- *Instruction and care sheet*

CHECK PRICE

Six-Sided Glass Terrarium for Succulents

This beautiful terrarium is about the size of the average flowerpot but much more elegant. Easy to handle and durable, it's the perfect home for succulents or air plants that grow vertically.

Key features:

- *Hinged roof for ventilation and watering*
- *Easy to remove glass top*
- *Careful detailing*
- *Compact design*

CHECK PRICE

DIY Terrarium Kit

Small and neat, this DIY terrarium kit lets you create a miniature indoor garden in a few simple steps. It includes a glass vessel with a lid, hydro-stones, soil, and moss.

Key features:

- Complete kit (except for the plants)
- Kid-friendly design

CHECK PRICE

Creativity for Kids Grow 'n Glow Terrarium

You're looking at one of the most accessible terrariums you can buy your kids. Everything's included, including potting mix, wheatgrass and chia seeds, and river stones. Suitable for age 6 and upwards.

Key features:

- *Easy to put together*
- *Design and instructions stimulate creativity*

CHECK PRICE

Asked Questions on Terrariums

Our most asked questions on terrariums we've received from the comments, in your emails, and messages. If you're still unsure about anything terrarium, do not hesitate to leave a comment below.

What is in a terrarium?

A terrarium is a miniature garden growing inside a transparent glass container. The plants and the soil in a terrarium release water vapor which condenses on the glass walls and returns the plants. Terrariums can be open or sealed.

How do you make a terrarium?

To make a terrarium you need to cover a jar with a thin layer of pebbles, add a thinner layer of activated charcoal, and some potting soil. You can then fix the plants into the soil, beginning with the largest one. Lastly, add pebbles and other decorative features.

How do terrariums work?

Terrariums hold plants and soil that release water vapor which then collects on the walls of the vessel and returns to the soil, recreating the circuit of water in nature. Meanwhile, a layer of activated charcoal keeps the water fresh. Sealed terrariums are self-sufficient while open ones require only watering.

How do I make a terrarium for free?

To make a terrarium, take a clean glass jar, fill the bottom with pebbles, add a bit of activated charcoal, and a thicker layer of soil. Fix a few tiny plants into the soil and add decorative elements or pebbles and some water. Seal the jar to keep the moisture inside or leave it open and water it regularly.

Happiness in a Terrarium

*Whether it's big or small, handmade or bought in a store, **a terrarium is a special, live object**. It may not be as busy as a vivarium or <u>planted aquarium</u>. But watching plants thrive in a **self-sufficient miniature ecosystem** that you created can be **deeply rewarding**. Buy a terrarium or build your own and you'll understand why!*

And bonus for you

20 Best Terrarium Plants for a Beautiful DIY Terrarium

*Are you a gardening enthusiast looking to **bring the outdoor gardens indoor**? Or a city slicker searching for a green relief from the concrete jungle around you? Terrarium plants are the perfect solution!*

*Terrariums, not to be confused with <u>jarrariums</u>, are **mini plant ecosystems growing in a glass jar**. They have taken the gardening world by storm, and it's easy to see why. One, they are low maintenance. Two, they can easily fit on a tabletop. And three, they make for a delightful addition to any home.*

*Terrariums, whether created with cacti, succulents, or tropical plants, are self-contained. This means that they're **pretty easy to care for**—provided you give them the right dose of sunshine and water. What's more, these miniature gardens can **thrive for years**!*

But before you fetch a glass jar and get your terrarium growing, you will want to choose the right plants for your mini-ecosystem. Read on to know more about it...

What Are Terrarium Plants?

Terrarium plants are small, **slow-growing plants** housed in a glass vessel. And if you're not adept at taking good care of houseplants, they are the ultimate shortcut to surrounding yourself with greenery.

Terrariums can make indoor spaces more lively and inviting. They are also quite versatile in size—you can either go big or stay minimalistic with them.

So, if you are a newbie, here are some **terrarium plant ideas** to help you get started:

- Use a diverse array of glass vessels like cloche, open globes, bulbs, and jars.
- Grow plants like ferns, carnivorous plants, air plants, and succulents in your terrarium. They can thrive in small, enclosed spaces.

- *Create eye-catching landscapes—from a mossy woodland and a whimsical fairy garden to a cacti desert and a tropical jungle.*
- *Add decorative pieces like seashells, glass pebbles, and driftwood to your little plant world.*

The Best Terrarium Plants

As a basic rule of thumb, the best terrarium plants are **petite and slow-growing**. You don't want them touching the sides of your vessel.

Other than that, there are endless terrarium plant options, so which to choose? Easy. Choosing the best terrarium plants will depend on **whether your terrarium is open or closed**.

Open terrariums are ideal for **plants that prefer dry conditions**. Succulents, air plants, and cacti thrive in them.

Closed terrariums have their own mini climate. They are best suited for **moisture and heat-loving plants** like ferns, mosses, and orchids.

Tip: Since your plants will be sharing a habitat, make sure they have similar light and moisture needs.

Open Terrarium Plants

Open terrariums are a great way for you to get started. They promote **better airflow for plants** and you don't have to worry about condensation issues. Plus, they have a **lower risk of mold and rot**.

Keep in mind that plants in open terrariums prefer a more arid environment. Such terrariums also work well for plants that need direct sunlight.

Here are some plants that thrive in open terrariums:

1. Air Plants (Tillandsia)

Air plants don't need soil to thrive. They attach themselves to a host for survival and absorb water and nutrients through their leaves. Not only do they make for a pretty addition to a terrarium, but they also purify the air!

Tip: You can place your air plant atop driftwood or use a flat stone as a base.

2. Succulents

<u>Succulents</u> are plants with thick, fleshy foliage. If you often forget to water your plants, then these plants are for you—they can thrive in scarce water. Many succulents stay small, allowing them to live for years in a terrarium without transplanting.

Tip: Overwatering your succulents will rot their roots. Water them only once a week.

3. Button Ferns (Pallaea Rotundifolia)

Button ferns are drought-tolerant, as opposed to the other members of the fern family. Because of their evergreen nature and beautiful round, leathery foliage, they have become a popular terrarium plant.

Tip: Button ferns prefer subdued light during the summer and bright, indirect light during winter.

4. Cacti

If you want to create a desert landscape in your terrarium, get cacti! These plants can't survive in closed terrariums with high humidity and bad airflow. So, make sure you have a medium to large opening in the container.

Note: *Cacti look amazing in open terrariums, but they don't survive very long. This is because the plants need regular airflow and low humidity to thrive.*

5. Jade Plant (Crassula Ovata)

Jade plants are generally manicured as <u>bonsais for terrariums</u>. Since they need frequent watering, an open terrarium is a good choice for them. A simple rule is to water your jade plants when the topsoil is just about dry.

Tip: Because jade plants are considered to be a symbol of good luck, place them atop your work table.

Closed Terrarium Plants

Closed terrariums are a bit more complicated to maintain. But they are **worth all your effort**. Because they are enclosed, they act more like tiny, self-sustaining gardens.

You can **build your closed terrarium using tropical plants** that love moisture and heat. Bear in mind that tropicals are going to eventually outgrow their vessel, so **you will need to transplant them**.

Here are some easy-going plants for a closed terrarium:

6. Peperomia (*Peperomia Pellucida*)

The Peperomia genus has low-growing, compact plants. Some are green-leaved while some have leaves that are blushed with white or red. These tropical plants thrive in humid conditions.

Note: There are over a thousand species in the Peperomia genus, so you have plenty of options to choose from!

7. Moss

Mosses and closed terrariums go together perfectly. That's because they are slow-growing and they thrive in moisture and low light. Plus, they don't take up much vertical space or contend with the other plants.

Tip: Carpeting mosses like java moss and feather moss are best for layering your terrarium, giving it a natural woodland look.

8. Nerve Plants (*Fittonia*)

Nerve plants are colorful tropical plants. They enjoy warm temperatures, high humidity, and partial to full shade.

Because these plants grow to a maximum height of 10 to 15 centimeters, they are perfect for the limited confines of a terrarium.

9. Ferns

Most ferns prefer to grow in the warm, moist environment of a closed terrarium. Lemon button fern and maidenhair fern are two popular small-growing ferns. Grow them to add volume to your terrarium.

Tip: Pruning your ferns regularly will encourage them to grow fuller.

10. Polka Dot Plant (Hypoestes Phyllostachya)

Daub cheer to your terrarium with the delightful polka dot plant. This warmth- and moisture-loving plant is dappled with pink, purple, red, or white on green leaves.

Note: Under favorable conditions, the plant makes tiny lavender-colored flowers in the summer.

Small Terrarium Plants

Small terrarium plants are truly small plants, and not just the immature versions of larger plants. With their small leaves and small growth habit, they are perfect to grow in your terrarium.

With minimal care, they will continue to look pretty and not outgrow the space. Here are a few small terrarium plants to look at:

11. Strawberry Begonia (*Saxifraga Stolonifera*)

Strawberry begonias make for the perfect terrarium plants. Why? Because they do not grow taller than 8 inches. And in late spring, they produce tiny, white, star-shaped flowers.

12. Miniature Orchids

It's a joy to watch mini orchids bloom in a terrarium! The plant typically prefers warm and humid conditions. So closed terrariums suit them well.

Tip: Miniature jewel orchid and miniature phalaenopsis are the easiest types of orchids for your closed terrarium.

13. Miniature English Ivy (*Hedera Helix*)

The miniature version of the English ivy has tiny, pointed, dark green leaves. The vine is petite and easy-to-grow. It will creep across the base of the terrarium and can serve as ground cover.

Tip: The plant is small-leaved and grows less vigorously than other types of ivy. But you will have to prune it regularly.

14. Baby's Tears (*Soleirolia Soleirolii*)

This plant has small rounded leaves that need frequent pruning. It forms mats of tiny, vividly green leaves, making it an ideal ground cover plant. The plant will stay small and can be tucked into any terrarium.

15. Bonsai

Bonsais can be planted in both open and closed terrariums. Their reduced root systems and diminutive habit make them ideal terrarium plants. Tropical species like ficus or aralia will thrive in a closed terrarium.

Tip: Bonsais do best when given a little fresh air once in a while.

Large Terrarium Plants

Large terrarium plants are suitable for planting in open or large terrariums. Bear in mind that these plants will need frequent pruning to prevent them from growing out of the terrarium.

Terrariums featuring large plants demand extra work, but they are totally worth it. Not only are they rare, but they also make your garden-in-a-glass stand out.

Take a look at these large terrarium plants:

16. Spider Plant (*Chlorophytum Comosum*)

Spider plants *have long, narrow, green and white striped leaves that can add bling to your terrarium. The plant is terrarium-friendly and thrives in high humidity.*

Tip: Keep an eye out for those little plantlets that the plant makes. Remove them from the terrarium before they take over the whole thing.

17. Venus Flytrap (*Dionaea Muscipula*)

Because of its wetland and marshy history, venus flytrap will thrive in the humid conditions of a terrarium. Plant in moss, add a little sand and leaf mold, keep it moist, and give it full sun to bring out its deep red hues.

18. Golden Pothos (*Epipremnum Aureum*)

This climbing plant is arguably the easiest to grow in a terrarium, even if you forget to water it now and then. It has beautiful heart-shaped yellow, white, or pale green leaves.

While it prefers warmth and moisture, it is an extraordinarily versatile plant that can tolerate different growing conditions.

Tip: The vine is a vigorous grower, and you will have to prune it to keep it in check.

19. Croton (*Codiaeum Variegatum*)

Croton is a vibrant-hued plant that can be a fantastic addition to your terrarium. The plant desires light and works particularly well in open terrariums.

20. Prayer Plant (*Maranta Leuconeura*)

The plant got its name because it folds up the leaves every night, as if in prayer. It likes to be warm and well-watered and can grow to be 12 inches tall.

Tip: You will know if the plant is not getting enough light—its leaves will stay folded even during the day.

Caring for Terrarium Plants

*Properly planted terrarium plants are **pretty much self-sustaining**. But some care and attention, especially in the first couple of months, can go a long way.*

Here are some points to remember:

Terrarium Light

*Too much sunlight can burn the plant leaves and stems. But too little sunlight leads to mush. It's best to **expose your terrarium plants to bright, indirect light**.*

Tip: You can rotate the terrarium regularly to ensure even sunlight exposure.

Air Ventilation in a Terrarium

Ventilate your closed terrarium every now and then to let some fresh air in. Doing so will also protect your mini-garden from molds that grow due to over-humidity.

Tip: Air your terrarium during the day and cover it during the night.

Watering Terrariums

An enclosed terrarium requires little or no watering. It recycles its own water. An open terrarium may want watering once a week in small doses. Use a syringe, eyedropper, or misting spray to avoid over-watering.

Tip: Shriveled leaves? Time to water. Yellowing or mushy leaves? You're over-watering.

Pruning

There is nothing worse than an overcrowded terrarium where plants are fighting for space. Therefore, prune regularly. Remove spent flowers and leaves. Do not decompose the plant parts in the container—it may cause fungal infections.

Fertilizing

Most terrariums do not need any fertilizer. But if your plants start to appear malnourished, fertilize them sparingly. In a terrarium, the last thing you want is to stimulate rapid growth!

Tip: When fertilizing, use a weak mixture (one-fourth strength) of an all-purpose houseplant food.

Cleaning

Keep the container clean by wiping off debris, both inside and out. Dirty or foggy glass will make it harder for light to reach your plants. Also, clean the decorative pieces as they may gather algae or fungus.

Tip: Do not use strong cleaning products on the inside of the terrarium. They may damage your plants.

Where to Buy Terrarium Plants

Terrarium plants have been in vogue for a few years now. With their ever-increasing popularity, just about every garden center, nursery, and florist shop has them on display.

But if you do not have any luck there, or are looking for a better selection, you can easily find plenty of stores online offering a fabulous range of terrarium plants.

If you are planning to buy terrarium plants, give these options a go:

Terrarium & Fairy Garden Plants

You will find plants like Red Polka Dot Plant, Sansevieria Hahnii, Furcrlaera, Baby Rubber Plant, and Parlour Palm. A set includes seven to eight terrarium and fairy garden plants of approximately 4 to 6 inches.

CHECK PRICE

Mini Terrarium Plants

Miniature plants like Friendship Plant, Spider Fern, Golden Clubmoss, and Strawberry Begonia are terrarium-friendly. While selecting plants, make sure to choose ones that thrive in the same environment you will be creating.

CHECK PRICE

Climber Vine Terrarium Plant

Climbing vines offer the possibility to scape your terrarium vertically. They come in shades of green, red, and brown and can enliven any miniature garden. Some terrarium-loving vines include String of Pearls (Curio Rowleyanus), Wandering Jew (Tradescantia Zebrina), Lipstick Plant (Aeschynanthus Radicans), and Baby Tears (Soleirolia Soleirolii).

CHECK PRICE

Terrarium Plants FAQs

Where to buy terrarium plants?

You can start by looking for options at your local nursery. You can also shop for terrarium plants online.

How to make terrarium plants?

Making terrarium plants is both easy and fun. All you need is a glass container to hold your mini garden, some potting soil, and the plants you want to grow. Get creative by adding decorative pieces like pinecones, pebbles, and seashells to your terrarium!

What are terrarium plants?

Terrarium plants, in simple words, are small, slow-growing plants. This includes plants like Peperomia, Nerve Plant, and Pothos.

What are good terrarium plants?

Typically, good terrarium plants should be petite. And they should have slow growth. You do not want them to touch the sides of your container. Succulents, ferns, and air plants are ideal to grow in your terrarium.

Gardening Under a Glass

If you do not have enough time, space, or energy to raise indoor plants, gardening under a glass is for you. Terrariums, with their bed of mosses, leafy plants, vines, and barks, can **add life to your home decor**.

You can also gift self-made terrariums to your loved ones. Doing so not only promotes sustainability—the gifts themselves are meaningful, symbolizing life and hope.

What's more, these mini-ecosystems, much like [planted aquariums](), are jam-packed with therapeutic benefits. They work as **natural humidifiers** and **purify the air**. Plus, taking care of tiny plants in a glass jar is a joy, wouldn't you agree?

Now if you have that itch to create something you could call your own, **get started with gardening under a glass!**

Made in United States
North Haven, CT
27 February 2022